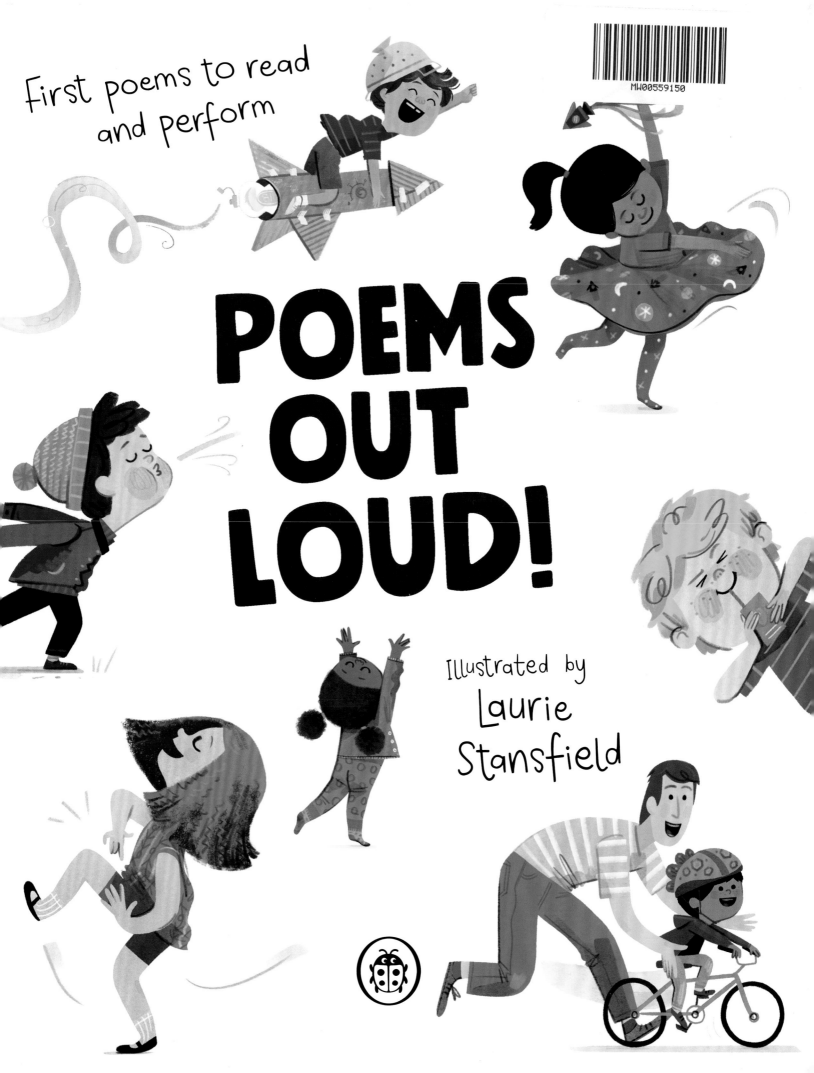

First poems to read and perform

POEMS OUT LOUD!

Illustrated by Laurie Stansfield

LADYBIRD BOOKS is part of the Penguin Random House group of companies whose addresses can be found at global.penguinrandomhouse.com.

www.penguin.co.uk   www.puffin.co.uk   www.ladybird.co.uk

Penguin
Random House
UK

First published 2019
001

A CIP catalogue record for this book is available from the British Library
Printed in China
ISBN: 978–0–241–37070–4

All correspondence to:
Ladybird Books, Penguin Random House Children"s
80 Strand, London WC2R 0RL

Contents

Upside Down

Whenever I stand on my feet, I suppose
That the thinks that I've thought simply sink to my toes.
Now, a think is no good when it falls to your foot,
As it goes to your toes and then sticks and stays put.
Once it's drained from your brain then a think won't return.
So the way to remember the things that you learn
And the thinks that you've thought and the books that you've read
Is to stand all day on your head, instead.

Elli Woollard

Angry

I was . . .

angry as a roaring lion,
angry as a swooping bat,

angry as a squawking parrot,
angry as a screeching cat,

angry as a hissing viper,
angry as a hopping frog,

angry as a big gorilla,
angry as a charging hog,

angry as a howler monkey,
angry as a barking mutt;

Yes I was very, VERY angry
when they said the zoo

was shut.

Joshua Seigal

Shoo, Fly, Shoo!

If a fly comes by and bothers you,
these are some of the things you can do.
You can trap it, or zap it, or give it a slap.
You can creep up behind it when it's taking a nap.
You can shout GET OUT! and hope that it goes.
You can whack it with a bat when it lands on Dad's nose.
You can introduce it to a hungry spider,
or launch an attack with a paper glider.
You can show it the door and wave goodbye,
or hope it meets up with another fly.
But if all else fails and the fly flies away,
sit down, relax, and have a nice . . .
GOTCHA!

Brian Moses

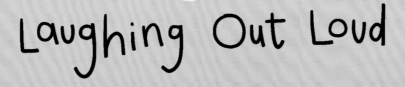

Laughing Out Loud

There is nothing I love more
than laughter. Giggles escaping through snorts,
it sounds like love.
I wonder what laughter looks like
inside my body.
I think it starts deep
in the tummy.
The colour red, taking up space.
It kind of feels like I'm full from lunch or
like butterflies or an earthquake.
Then it moves up,
filling my chest. It feels like
popping candy now.
A loud orange. It's warm too.
The best of laughs looks like a stream of
bubbles escaping your nose.
Then comes the pressure, forcing
the sound out of your mouth.
It's the brightest yellow now and
sounds like musical notes.
It gets you in trouble
when you are at school,
when you are at the dentist,
when you are pretending to be asleep –
there is no way to control
the giggles.
If you do,
it's like locking colour away in a box
and who would want to do that?

Amina Jama

Pirates

A pirate has an eye patch
and just one pirate leg,
a pirate has a pirate parrot
who sits on her pirate head.

A pirate wears a pirate hat
and sails the seven seas,
she sails on a pirate ship
sipping pirate tea.

She has a shaky pirate crew
who shiver when she shouts,
she holds a mighty pirate sword
that she likes to wave about.

She's hunting for the pearl crown
that the mermaid-boys sunk,
she's seeking out the starfish town
hidden in a shipwrecked trunk.

And when the pirate treasure is found
and polish put on each pirate's leg,
she gives each member of her pirate crew
a pat upon their pirate head.

Joseph Coelho

The Beetle

Shiny, black and super fast,
I see a beetle scuttle past.

I stop it with my hand to see
If a beetle can be as clever as me!

I want to watch its wings unfold,
Because some beetles can fly, or so I've been told.

But once in the air it gets stuck in my hair.
I definitely do not want it there!

Now up so close and cheek to cheek,
I discover this little beetle can speak!

Some people might find beetles scary . . .
But *I* can tell you they're garden fairies!

The bugs that live where your garden grows
Are more than they seem when you're nose to nose.

Wearing a wonderful range of disguises,
In different colours, shapes and sizes,

They dress this way to keep their fairy kingdom hidden,
But they rarely tell us because it's forbidden.

For imagine if everyone were to know
That fairies live where the flowers grow!

Nadine Wild-Palmer

Do You See Me?

Hey you,
Come closer
Tell me

What does my nose look like?
A shiny bubble.

What of my eyes?
Juicy apples.

My lips?
A magical bouncy castle.

My ears?
Two golden trumpets.

And my chin?
A glowing birthday present.

My hair?
Sweet icing on a cake.

My eyebrows?
A warm soft cuddle.

Now tell me what my forehead looks like?
A bright endless sky.

Caleb Femi

Drums on Legs

When I'm dancing
I forget everything.
The beat takes me over

I sing
I'm the singer
I strum the air
I'm the lead guitar
Ba bum bum bum
I'm the bass
But most of all
I'm the drummer

I'm the drums
Drums on legs
The drums
Drums on legs
The drums
Drums on legs
The drums
Drums on legs
The drums
Drums on legs
The drums
Drums on legs.

When the music stops
It's so quiet
I can hear myself
Sweating.

Roger McGough

The Elephant in the Classroom

An elephant came to my classroom one day.
He sat at my table and wanted to play.
My teacher said, "Shoo! All the children are scared!"
But the elephant stayed where he was, in my chair.

The caretaker came with his bucket and broom.
"I'll sweep the elephant out of the room!"
He pushed him and pulled him – "You shouldn't be there!"
But the elephant stayed where he was, in my chair.

The head teacher came in and read him a speech
about elephants being too awkward to teach
and not knowing the rules. But he just didn't care:
the elephant stayed where he was, in my chair.

Camera teams came from the BBC news.
"Want to be in a feature," they asked him,
"on zoos? Want to be in *Celebrity Animals*? Yeah?"
But the elephant stayed where he was, in my chair.

Next day when we went in the classroom, he'd gone.
My teacher was pleased, and said now we'd get on
with spellings and maths, which was why we were there.
But I want that elephant back, in my chair!

Sheila Norton

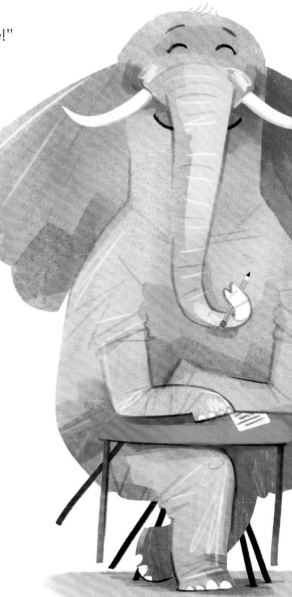

Bathtime

It's a bit of a laugh, in the bath

there's bubbles and squeaks
when I slide on both cheeks

toes in the tap
and a warm flannel slap

wrinkly skin
and shampoo on the chin

there's dancing about
when it's time to get out

it's a bit of a laugh, in the bath!

Matt Goodfellow

Grow UP!

Every day
in every way
I grow
a little more

Older, higher,
wider too –
and further
from the floor

My head,
my hands,
my knees,
my nose,
my teeth,
my tongue,
my toes . . .

So steadily
so silently
my body
slowly
GROWS!

James Carter

Two Left Shoes on Two Right Feet

Two left shoes
on two right feet,
walk downhill
up a one-way street.

One long glove
on a short left hand,
fingers outstretched
like worms in the sand.

Big woolly jumper
red and curvy
on upside down,
wearer topsy-turvy!

Grandma's pressie,
warm hat and scarf.
Don't fit now, though . . .
. . . shrunk in the barf!

John Rice

15

Night Songs

Who is it I hear and whose voice is that?
What are the things I can hear in the dark?

Hush now, just owl's song on pale wings of ash,
only the shadow of her beak so sharp.

Be still, just bat's song of chase and catch,
only an echo, for he cannot see far.

Don't fear, just moth's song when the moon is fat,
only her searching for a fallen star.

Listen, just badger's song of bulb and wasp,
only the shuffle of nose on soft earth.

There now, just hedgehog's song, all crunch and snap,
only snail silver on slippery paths.

No, just fox's song of broke fence and latch,
only lost feathers, no bite and no bark.

Sleep now, only my song, warm under thatch,
sweet rhymes of love for your lullaby heart.

Sue Hardy-Dawson

The Washing-Up Liquid Ignited

I built up a rocket
Of cardboard and tape,
Climbed right on board
And tried to escape,
With my bottle-top buttons,
And cardboard sides,
To keep me safe from alien eyes.
The washing-up liquid ignited, I flew!
Took a lap round the planet,
Stopped off at the Moon,
Ate a sandwich on Venus
And took in the view,
Posted letters to Mum
Saying I'd be home soon.
And when I landed
In time for my tea,
I told stories of space
That they didn't believe,
But I pulled from my pocket
A section of star
To prove to them all
That I'd travelled so far,
And after we'd eaten
I climbed back on board,
Reignited the washing-up liquid
And soared.

Jay Hulme

Spiders

Spiders are my worst nightmare –
they crawl around my ceiling;
they disappear throughout the day
and come back in the evening.

Sometimes they're small as moving dots.
Sometimes they're fat and slow.
Sometimes they're fast, with long, thin legs
or striped in brown and yellow.

I don't mind when they live outside
or hide away under rocks.
I just get scared if they're in my room –
what if they hide in my socks?

I know they can be tiny.
Mum says "But look at the size of you!"
She always frees them using a cup –
because spiders have lives, too.

One day I will be just as brave,
so brave, I'll think they're cool.
I might even save their lives myself
from the other kids at school.

Until then . . .

Spiders are my worst nightmare
when they crawl around my ceiling.
They disappear throughout the day
and come back in the evening.

Victoria Adukwei Bulley

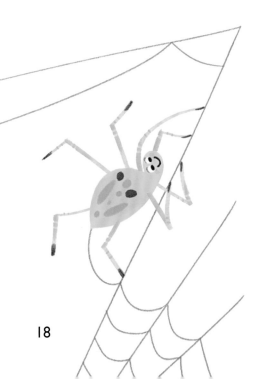

Two Wheels

Last week Dad said
He would teach me
How to ride my bike
But I've been riding bikes since I was TWO
And now I'm FIVE!

So that is what I told him.
I said,
"I DON'T NEED YOUR HELP!"
Mummy said, "Don't be so sure . . ."
(And told me not to yell).

So I said in my Sunday voice,
"Daddy, I CAN ride."
But Daddy said,
"I mean without those
        small wheels on the side."

"ARE YOU NUTS?!"
I shouted, "They're the things that keep me up!
Without them I would fall and bash my head
Or bruise my butt!"

"Well, that's why I'm here to help,"
Said Dad, all nice and calm,
"I'll be right beside you,
You won't come to any harm."

Mummy got some tools and took the little wheels off.
Daddy held the bike up and he said,
"Right, on you pop!"

Suddenly I took off and I didn't even fall
I was great
And I didn't need any help at all!

Ben Bailey Smith aka Doc Brown

Forwards and Backwards

I've heard of 10 green bottles
Hanging on the wall
I wish I was a cat with 9 lives
But what if I lost them all?
I once ate 8 berries
All in one go
I was weak for 7 days
When I had a bad cold
I saw a man play a guitar
Strumming 6 strings
Every day my 5 senses
Keep tingling
There are 4 seasons
Summer is my favourite
I eat 3 meals a day
Good food, I savour it
You have 2 ears
So please hear me out
This is 1 poem you can read
Forwards and backwards out loud!

Karl Nova

Shhh...

I know where Mum
Hides her chocolate biscuits

I'm not going to tell you
Because it's a secret

There were five in the packet
But now there are four

I wonder if she'll notice
If I just have one more?

Roger Stevens

Mr Bear

There's a mirror in our living room
and as I sit and stare,
it's so completely clear to me
I should have been a bear.

I'm way too small, I have no claws
and not a lot of hair.
There's been a terrible mistake –
I should have been a bear.

My hands are really tiny
and my teeth are hardly there.
I'm really not that frightening –
I should have been a bear.

Whoever made me look this way,
they clearly couldn't care.
I'm starting my new school today –
I should have been a bear.

What happens when I walk inside
and everybody stares?
My tiny growl will make them laugh –
I should've been a bear.

This really isn't fair at all,
does anybody care?
How will I defend myself?
I should've been a bear.

We're leaving now, my bag is packed,
I've chosen what to wear.
I guess it's really up to me . . .
so call me

Mr Bear.

**Steven Camden
aka Polarbear**

Song for Exploding Stars

You are an exploding star. Sparks into dark blue.

You are a firework. You are a solar system and the telescope
to watch the planets through.

You are the smell of spring. You are a whole row of sunflowers,
standing tall. You are the way the moon dips into water
and the echo of a bird's call.

You are flames. You are the way the fireflies glow.
You are thunderstorms and hilltops, all the colours of the rainbow.

You are waves crashing on a shore, you can be hurricanes.
You are ancient rivers and waterfalls. You are the gentle summer rain.

You are the perfect satsuma. You are the electric fizz of tangy sweets.
You are a thick slice of rich cake. You are a drink
of cold water in the heat.

You are the cheer when a goal is scored, when a ball makes a net shake.
You are an aeroplane soaring through the air.
You are a boat sailing on a lake.

You are the chorus of a song, the bass line and the beat.
You are clapping hands and shouts of joy.
You are the spotlight's heat.

You are a mathematic equation. You are whole libraries stacked tall.
You are stories and poems and myths and plays, the wonder of it all.

You are the vibrant city. You are all the pennies in the fountain.
You're skyscrapers and bridges, roads
that lead to the top of a mountain.

You are all the good things. Though it can be easy to forget,
fill up rooms with your brilliance, your voice
and don't you ever let

anyone tell you you're anything less than brilliant and bright.
You are the future, you are hope.
You are the sun bursting through the night.

And though there might be those in life who tell you that you're not,
you hold so much greatness in your palm, so don't you ever stop.

Cecilia Knapp

Big Fat Budgie

I'm a
big fat budgie

I don't do a lot.
Might park on my perch.
Might peck at my pot. Might peek
at my mirror. Might ring my bell.
Might peer through the bars
of my fat budgie cell.
Might say "Who's a pretty boy then?"
Might not.
I'm a
big fat
budgie.
I don't
do a
lot.

**Michaela
Morgan**

Can You Fly Like a Butterfly?

Can you fly like a butterfly?
Flick, flick, flick as you flutter by
Wings that fling you through the summer sky
Can you fly like a butterfly?

Can you swim like a giant whale?
Spin, spin, spin as you twist your tail
Flap your fin like an enormous sail
Can you swim like a giant whale?

Can you leap like a chimpanzee?
Swing, swing, swing – dance from tree to tree
Swish through leaves – an emerald treetop sea
Can you leap like a chimpanzee?

Can you glide like the eagles do?
Ride, ride, ride the waves of warm clear blue
Nothing up there quite as high as you
Can you glide like the eagles do?

Can you sleep till you start to dream?
Flick, spin, swing – ride a bright moonbeam
Up to a castle made from space ice cream
Can you sleep till you start to dream?

Joe Marriott

Pick a Sound, Any Sound

What's your favourite noise?
What's the best sound around?

What would you choose
from all the world's whoops
and fizzes
and gurgles
and BOOMS?

A space-rocket zoom
or popping balloons?

Tiger-cub sneezes or seaside breezes?

The honk of a goose,
a brilliant burp,
or the *slurp* of your straw with a last sip of juice?

It could be the *crunch* of a cornflake mid-munch.

Or
are yours
the sort
of ears
to cheer
the soft-as-silk sounds?

The swoosh of a cloud,
the shush of a secret,
the creak of trees,
hum of bees,
swish of a grasshopper rattling its knees.

Or the soft hush that hangs when everything STOPS.

So what do you think?
What's your favourite noise?
A raindrop's *plink*,
an ocean's roars,
a hippo's snores?

The choice (of course) is yours.

Kate Wakeling

Frances

Frances
dances
dances
every night.

Frances
dances
dances
every day.

Frances
dances
dances
of delight.

Frances'
neighbours
wish she'd
go away.

A.F. Harrold

The Dormouse

The dormouse likes
round berries to eat
and nibbles round holes
in his round nut treats

he wiggles his ears
and patters his toes
trembles his whiskers
round his round nose

sleeps for months
in a round grass bed
tail curling round
his nose and head

he squeaks when awake
then sleeps so sound
he's a *snore*mouse
half the year round!

Liz Brownlee

Braving the Sea

My feet are in
I think I'll freeze!
Now my ankles,
Now my knees.

Should I dive now,
Like I planned?
Or should I run
Back to dry land?

It feels too cold,
I don't feel brave,
OH NO – too late!
A monster wave!

Philip Waddell

Milo the Leaf Blower

Milo is a Leaf Blower,
He blows every single leaf,
They spin and twirl and hit the ground –
He catches three leaves in his teeth.

The golden leaves lie in a pile,
They cover Milo's nose –
No matter how much Milo blows
They pile up on his toes.

Milo blows and blows the leaves,
The orange and the red,
But if the wind blows north to west –
They pile up on his head!

Chrissie Gittins

Night in the Ocean

Night kisses me to sleep and I dream of the sea.
Salty waves wash me clean,
the ocean becomes the biggest bath in the world
and I bob, up and down
gently, softly.

Every night
I dream I am a mermaid
with salt and sand in my hair
and a tail covered in golden scales.
They shimmer and sparkle under a moon
that is full and big.

I swim with the fish I have made friends with.
We are all different,
none of us shine the same,
but we all glitter when we dance.

And every morning when I open my eyes, I smile.
Because at night I am a mermaid
who dances with the fish under a full moon,
and swims for miles and miles.

Abigail Cook

Bedtime Rhymes

This little poem I'm taking to bed,
Letting its words skip around in my head,
Kicking its rhymes to and fro in my mind:
This little poem is one of a kind.

This little poem they can't take away,
No one can tell me a poem can't play.
My toys may be tidied; my light may be out,
But this little poem will still dance about.

This little poem I cuddle and keep
And muddle the words when I'm falling asleep.
Happy rhymes rolling around in my head:
This little poem's curled up in my bed.

Celia Warren